Charles Mather Cooke

Speech of Hon. Chas. M. Cooke,

Delivered in the Dr. Grissom Trial for the Defence, Thursday, July 18, 1889

Charles Mather Cooke

Speech of Hon. Chas. M. Cooke,
Delivered in the Dr. Grissom Trial for the Defence, Thursday, July 18, 1889

ISBN/EAN: 9783744786195

Printed in Europe, USA, Canada, Australia, Japan

Cover: Foto ©ninafisch / pixelio.de

More available books at **www.hansebooks.com**

SPEECH

OF

HON. CHAS. M. COOKE,

DELIVERED IN THE

DR. GRISSOM TRIAL,

FOR THE DEFENCE,

THURSDAY, JULY 18, 1889.

RALEIGH, N. C.:

EDWARDS & BROUGHTON, STEAM PRINTERS AND BINDERS.

1889.

SPEECH

OF

HON. CHAS. M. COOKE,

DELIVERED IN THE

DR. GRISSOM TRIAL,

FOR THE DEFENCE,

THURSDAY, JULY 18, 1889.

RALEIGH, N. C.:

EDWARDS & BROUGHTON, STEAM PRINTERS AND BINDERS.

1889.

HON. CHAS. M. COOKE,

Delivered in the Dr. Grissom Trial, Thursday, July 18, 1889.

Mr. President and Gentlemen of the Board: When it was
rumored some weeks ago that this Board had been called
together in extra session, for the purpose of hearing charges
which were to be preferred against some officer of the North
Carolina Insane Asylum, it produced anxiety in the public
mind. There was no certainty as to the officer, nor was there
any specification as to the charges; and when, a few days after-
ward, it was published that the charges were to be preferred
against the Superintendent of the Institution, it filled the
people of the State with a sad surprise.

There was still uncertainty as to the character of the
charges; and when, at the commencement of this trial, the
charges were preferred, alleging that the Superintendent of
this Institution had been guilty—first, of gross immorality
in connection with certain female attendants and others of
this Institution; and, secondly, with mismanagement of, and
cruelty to, the patients under his charge; and, thirdly, that
he had been guilty of misappropriating the property of the
Institution, they were of so serious a nature that the people
of North Carolina, notwithstanding their previous notice,
were not prepared for them. They cried out, "Is it possible
that this man, to whom we have for so many years given our
confidence, has been guilty of these things? Has this man,
who is the husband of a good and virtuous wife, stooped to
attempt to defile another man's bed? Has this father of
daughters debauched the widow's daughter? and for the
gratification of his own wicked lusts has he been at the vile
work of attempting to compass the ruin of young girls who
were attendants in this Institution? and all this under the
same roof that covers his own wife and daughters? Is it

possible that this man, who has always been brave, when he
was facing men, who has been courageous in every conflict,
who wears upon his body the fearful scars of an honorable
war, has been so cowardly as to cruelly mistreat those who,
by reason of their weakness, are under his charge? Is it
possible that he who has had fame on account of his gen-
erosity, who has been almost prodigal in his personal lib-
erality, who has ever been quick to respond to the call of
charity, has laid his hand upon the property of this Institution to appropriate it to his own use? Can it be that he is a
libertine? Can it be that he is a cruel tyrant? Can it be
that he, with his great intellect and his proud record, has
passed under the control and influence of the demon of
avarice?

But these charges have been preferred, and for three weeks
you have been engaged in trying the question as to whether
or not this man, who has for nearly a quarter of a century
occupied such a high and honorable position in the history
of North Carolina, be guilty thereof. You have heard the
evidence, and the counsel are now engaged in discussing
the same, before you shall come to your final determination.

Before I proceed further, it gives me pleasure to commend,
in the highest terms, the ability, the fairness, the impartiality,
which have characterized your deliberations; and for myself
and my associates, I tender you our grateful appreciation of
the kindness and courtesy you have shown to us. Whatever
may be the result of this trial, your patience and your gen-
erous consideration towards all the parties engaged herein
will be gratefully remembered and cherished.

This case, like cases in the courts of law, is to be tried
upon evidence. This is settled by the language of the statute which endows you with the power of this trial, for it
makes your conduct to depend upon proof.

It would be well if we could settle now the question of the
sufficiency of proof that should be required for a conviction
in this trial. There are three rules which apply in courts of

law, depending for their difference upon the nature of the action tried. First, in all criminal actions the rule of sufficiency of proof is, that the jury must be satisfied, beyond a reasonable doubt, to justify a conviction; second, in civil cases, generally, the rule is, that he who holds the affirmative of an issue must maintain it by a preponderance of evidence, or else he is not entitled to recover; and, thirdly, there is another rule which applies in cases where the *bona fides* of a transaction are sought to be impeached, as where there is an issue of fraud, or where public officers are clothed with the exercise of their public duties, and the issue is as to whether or not they have used more power upon the subjects of their jurisdiction than was legally allowed, and that rule is, that the issue shall not be found in the affirmative except upon clear proof; that is, unless the triers are satisfied.

I shall not insist upon the application of the first-named rule to this case—that is, that you should be satisfied beyond a reasonable doubt before you find the respondent guilty upon these charges; but I do insist that the last-named rule should govern in this case, and that you should not find the respondent guilty upon any one of these charges, except ·upon full proof, which is the language of the statute authorizing this trial, and I now ask the counsel upon the other side if they will not agree with me that it is the proper rule for this? The counsel say that they do. So, we will consider that as settled.

The prosecution has introduced its evidence upon these charges, and the respondent has introduced his evidence in reply thereto, but the counsel for the prosecution, who addressed you on yesterday, made no allusion whatever, in his long and able speech, to the first and third charges, but confined himself entirely to the discussion of the evidence upon the second charge—that is, the one of cruel treatment of the patients. He has tendered us battle upon that issue alone. Am I to understand that, upon their consciences, after all the evidence is in, they have come to the conclusion that they would not be justified in pressing this Board for a conviction upon the first and third charges? And before proceeding further, I would be glad to be advised by the gentlemen who represent the prosecution, if it is their purpose to abandon the first and third charges

They reply that they do not abandon the first charge; that they shall insist that the respondent is guilty thereof. And in relation to the third charge, that while they think the evidence has been sufficient to show that there has been a misappropriation of the property of the Institution by the respondent, still, on account of the insignificant value thereof, they do not attach much importance to it. I have great respect for the gentleman (Col. Waddell) who, speaking for the prosecution, has made this, which he calls frank, confession in respect to the third charge, and no man in North Carolina would appreciate more than I would an honorable, frank concession from him; but when he proposes a concession which would only affect the extent of the property taken, and in no way decrease the moral turpitude of my client, then I spurn the concession.

I must decline, just now, the tender of battle made by the gentleman yesterday. Later on, in my remarks, I shall attempt to reply to his speech.

I shall begin the discussion with the evidence upon the first charge, for the reason, first, that it is orderly to do so; and secondly, for that it is the most important one, and of greater concern to the respondent, in that it most seriously affects his character and happiness. Under this charge there are five specifications, and we shall consider them in the order in which they are written.

The first is, that the respondent has been guilty of illicit intercourse with Miss Nora Burch. We will now consider the evidence upon this specification:

Plummer King, for the prosecution, testifies that in July or August of last year, standing on the corner of the stage at the further end of this hall, he saw Miss Nora Burch come up the southern steps, go along this hall and go into the matron's sitting-room, which is at the extreme end of this hall from the stage ; that when she went into the room, she left the door ajar to the extent of some two or three inches, and that some three minutes thereafter, Dr. Grissom came up the northern steps, and went into the same room and closed the door, and not long thereafter he (King) came down the stage steps, went along the hall to the door of the matron's bed-room, opening into the hall, and peeped through the key-hole, and saw Dr. Grissom and Miss Burch on a single-bed in that room, with their feet towards the door, in sexual intercourse. He further stated, that this was on Saturday afternoon, and that he was on the stage at that time in compliance with the directions of Mrs. Lawrence, the matron, for the purpose of ascertaining what repairs were needed to the stage scenery thereon ; that he found that one of the screens had fallen down, and that it would be necessary to fasten it by cleats to the wall ; that he did not do the work on Saturday afternoon, but returned on Monday and did the work. He said there was no one else on the stage but himself. He did not, on his first examination, either on direct or cross-examination, say that he saw Emanuel Jones, or any one else, in the hall or on the floor while Dr. Grissom and Miss Burch were in that room.

Jones, the next witness, testified that, on the same day, he came up the steps to the floor on which is the matron's room, and, standing at the head of the steps, he saw Miss Burch go across the passage and enter the sitting-room door. He says he then turned to the right and went into the chapel by the end door, and went across the chapel and took a position by the side-door which opens into the hall opposite the matron's sitting-room, and from that position he saw Dr. Grissom come up the steps into the hall and go into the matron's sitting-room, and not long thereafter he, the witness, moved across the hall, looked through the key-hole into the matron's bed-room, and saw the act of sexual intercours between Dr. Grissom and Miss Burch. He further testified, that he didn't tell of this in some time afterwards, and that the first one he told it to was the witness King, and that he afterwards told it to one of the prosecutors. He said he did not see Mr. King on the stage or on the floor or peeping through the key-hole. He says that some time ago he was walking on the street in the city of Raleigh, after dark, and some young white man whom he did not know called to him and told him that he was wanted up in Mr. Whitaker's office; said he did not know Mr. Whitaker, and did not know what he wanted with him, but that he went up into Mr. Whitaker's office and there made to Mr. Whitaker, who took it down in writing, the same statement, in substance, as his testimony in this trial.

After this, King was recalled by the prosecution, and testified that while he was standing on the corner of the stage, and before he peeped through the key-hole, he saw Emanuel Jones come out of the chapel, go across the hall and peep through the key-hole into the matron's bed-room, and that as soon as Jones had recrossed the hall and gone back into the chapel, he, the witness, came down the steps of the stage and went directly to the key-hole and discovered this intercourse between Dr. Grissom and Miss Burch. He said he looked for at least a half minute, and that the intercourse continued until he left. King also testified that he sometime ago informed the prosecutors of what he had seen.

This is all the evidence the prosecution offered upon this specification, except the testimony of Capt. West, who said that some time last fall or winter, he saw Dr. Grissom and Miss Burch go into the matron's sitting-room, and that fact could hardly be relied upon as any evidence of their guilty connection in the July or August preceding, nor any evidence of their guilty connection on the day testified to, since they went into the sitting-room which was at all times open to the inmates of the Institution.

Now let us consider the testimony of the defence on this specification :

Dr. Grissom testified that he never had any improper relations with Miss Nora Burch, and that he never made any improper advances to her, and he denied specifically the fact of intercourse as testified to by King and Jones. He further testified, that Miss Nora Burch was for several years an attendant at this Institution, and that she suffered with a disease peculiar to her sex, and that sometimes required local examination and treatment ; that these examinations were made in the matron's bed-room. That Miss Burch, to relieve the pain resulting from this trouble, became addicted to the use of morphine, and that this habit produced mental derangement or mania, which first discovered itself in February of this year. That Miss Burch was then moved into the matron's room, where she could be under the personal supervision of Mrs. Lawrence, the matron. That Dr. E. Burke Haywood was called in to see her and made her several visits. Dr. Fuller, first assistant physician of the Institution, also visited her. The mother of Miss Burch was notified of her condition by the witness, and came down and attended her for a good part of her sickness. Her condition did not improve, and she was sent to the Insane Asylum at Morganton, her home in Guilford County being within the prescribed limits of territory from which patients are to be sent to that asylum.

Mrs. Lawrence testified that she remembers well the occasion when King repaired the stage scenery at her request, and she said that the following are the circumstances : That King, who was the carpenter of the Institution, was doing some work in a room in one of the wards on the same floor with the hall, and that she went to him and informed him that one of the screens on the stage had fallen, and that she desired him to place it back ; that he went at once to the hall, she accompanying him ; that he, without leaving the room and without leaving the stage, completed the work that she requested him to do, and then came off the stage and went down the stairs, off the floor. She said that she was present with him during the whole time that he was on the stage or in the hall, and that she directed him in the making of the repairs, and that the work was accomplished within a half hour. She further testified, that during the summer of last year, the iron bedstead in her room did not sit in such a position that the foot thereof could be seen by a person looking through the key-hole. She further testified, that she never left the Institution on Saturday, for that on that day of the week she was engaged in inspecting and repairing the clothing of the patients. She said that Miss Nora Burch, who was, at the time of the alleged intercourse, the chief attendant in this Institution, was, in her bearing and conduct, a lady, and that she never saw any improper conduct on Dr. Grissom's part towards her.

Miss McKoy, who is now and has been for some time an attendant here, testified that on the occasion last summer when King made the repairs to the scenery on the theatrical stage, she was in the sewing-room, which adjoins the stage, the door of the room next to the stage was open, and that she knows, from her own personal observation, that Mrs. Lawrence came upon the stage with King, and remained with him during the time he was making the repairs, and until he left the floor and went down the steps; that her business in the Institution requires her to spend much of her time in that sewing-room, and that she, neither before nor after that time, saw King upon that stage.

I have stated substantially, and I trust fairly, the evidence on each side in respect to this specification. Now let us consider the value of this testimony. Let it be remembered that witnesses have testified to the good character of W. P. King; that many witnesses have come down from High Point, the home of Miss Nora Burch, and testified to her high character, and witnesses, coming from different sections of the State, and occupying high positions with respect to public confidence, and several of them ministers of God's gospel of truth and justian, have testified to the high character of Dr. Eugene Grissom, and among these latter have been those who have been inmates of this Institution, and who have experienced his kindness and the benefits of his treatment during the hours of their darkness and suffering. It can hardly be necessary for me to call the attention of the members of this Board, as evidence to the high character of Dr. Grissom, that for twenty-one years he has held this high position, from which you are now asked to depose him, and that he has filled it with great acceptability to the people of the State.

The witness King is discredited by the fact that the examination and investigation by Mr. Ashley discovered that it was physically impossible for a person occupying any position on that stage to have seen the door entering from the hall into the matron's sitting-room, and this view members of this Board are able to confirm by personal inspection, which they have made. He is further discredited by the fact that, when first examined as a witness, he failed to state that he saw Emanuel Jones when he peeped through that key-hole, when the importance of corroborating himself must have been apparent to him at that time. Again, I submit that it is improbable that Emanuel Jones should have come up the steps upon the floor, and walked into the chapel, passing within a few feet of where King alleges he was standing upon the stage, without seeing the witness King, and without the latter seeing him.

And even if this were so, is it not certain that if Emanuel Jones came out of that chapel and went across the hall and peeped into that key-hole, as both King and himself testified that he did, and then recrossed the hall back to the chapel, that he would have seen King, if he had been standing in that position? for it is true that persons who are going to peep through key-holes, conscious that it is discreditable and dishonorable, would be watchful to see if they were observed. And if King had occupied the position at that time that he said he occupied, then Jones had need only to turn his eye to the left in going, or to the right in returning, and he would have discovered King.

Another thing which is unexplained, by King, and which goes to his discredit, is that he says that he remained upon the stage after he had satisfied himself by personal inspection of the repairs that were needed. Why did he not go then? What kept him there? The suggestion that his attention was attracted and his suspicion aroused by seeing Miss Burch go across the hall into the matron's sitting-room cannot avail, for the matron's sitting-room was not a private room, but was open to all the attendants and the convalescent patients, and it was the duty of Miss Nora Burch, as chief attendant, to go there; and, according to the testimony of witness himself, at least three minutes elapsed after Miss Burch went into that room before Dr. Grissom came up the steps; and that the witness remained in that position on the stage with nothing to do and no purpose, is improbable and unreasonable.

He admitted in his testimony that by an order of this Institution neither he nor any of the other outside attendants were allowed upon this floor except upon orders for business, and as soon as the business was transacted to retire from this floor.

Then, is it not true, generally, that a man who admits that he derived his information by peeping through a key-hole, impeaches himself? His consciousness of this led him in the attempt to justify his conduct to give a reason which was absurd and disingenious; for he says he peeped through the key-hole to see what Dr. Grissom and Miss Burch were doing, because Dr. Grissom directed him to keep a look-out for any improper conduct between the male and female attendants of the Institution, and if he made any such discoveries to report to him. He is further impeached by his written statement, signed and given to Dr. Grissom, that he had never heard of any immoral conduct on the part of Dr. Grissom.

Why, if this man were truthful and brave, as is claimed for him by the prosecution, did he not, when interrogated by Dr. Grissom, in relation to what he had seen or heard of any immoral or improper conduct on his part towards any of the attendants or patients of this Institution, state to him frankly that he had witnessed the sinful intercourse between him and Miss Burch, which he has testified to on this stand?

He is impeached by the fact that he did not give information to Dr. Fuller, who was second in command of this Institution, or to any one else, until a short while ago, when he stated it to the prosecutors in this case.

Was this fact, of which he had knowledge, by personal observation, and which he knew proved the unfitness of the Superintendent of this Institution for this high position, so unimportant and so insignificant? or, was there no person of his acquaintance to whom, either from a sense of duty, or from a desire, common to human nature, to discover at least to somebody a piece of startling information, that he could unbosom himself? and must he, and did he, carry that secret in his own breast for months? That is improbable. Or if there were reasons that he should keep this secret for months, what reason is suggested for his telling it to the prosecutors afterwards?

Let us next consider what reliance is to be placed upon the testimony of Emanuel Jones, the colored servant. Do you believe him when he says that he came up those steps, and, standing at the head of the stair-way, saw Miss Nora Burch enter the matron's sitting-room? Gentlemen of the Board, you are sitting within a few feet of the position which the witness said he occupied, at the head of that stair-way, and you can see now, if it had not been proven to you before, that no range of vision of a person occupying that position could strike within twenty feet of that door. In order for Jones to have seen that door, it would have been necessary for him to have come to a position in this hall in front of the stage, and then he would have seen King, and King certainly would have seen him; and King testified that he did not see him until he came out of the chapel. Did he, too, know this great secret, and keep it for several months? Was there not among the attendants of this Institution, or elsewhere, some friend of his own race to whom he was willing to unbosom himself? And please notice, that after giving the information to King, we next find him giving this information to one of the prosecutors; then we find him in the office of Mr. Whitaker, at Raleigh, in the night-time, and there upon the invitation of a man he never saw, giving this secret, which he had locked up in his breast for many months, against his most intimate friends, to a gentleman whom he did not know.

I shall not allow this opportunity to pass without my saying that I deprecate this last method of attempting to destroy the character of a gentleman who has hitherto held a high position among his fellow-men, and the reputation of a woman who has been among her neighbors and friends as a pure and chaste maiden, by interrogating a colored menial servant of the household, as to what he had witnessed of the conduct of his employers by peeping through key-holes! Is the reputation of our manhood for integrity, and of our womanhood for chastity, to depend on such as this? If so, God help us!

The counsel for the prosecution deny that there is any conspiracy formed against Dr. Grissom, but they cannot deny that Dr. Rogers has now, and had before this prosecution commenced, very strong feelings against Dr. Grissom, and that his great interest and activity in this prosecution have been inspired by this feeling, and the letter written by him to one of his unfortunate female friends discovers upon its face that he was deeply anxious for the conviction of Dr. Grissom upon these charges; that he regarded it as a per-

sonal issue between himself and Dr. Grissom, and he thinks
to make his influence over this woman of some avail by
suggesting to her the evidence that she should furnish to
help him to secure the conviction of Dr. Grissom. This is
sufficient to affect the credibility of a witness, who admits
to a state of facts that shows that he has been, to any extent,
under the influence of Dr. Rogers in respect to his conduct
as a witness in this trial.

It may be safely assumed that Dr. Rogers procured the
attendance of the witness Jones at the office of the attorney
on the night above referred to. The negro, according to his
own admission, had previously had a conversation with Dr.
Rogers in respect to the matter, and he told the attorney in
Raleigh, on the night in question, just what Dr. Rogers
desired him to tell, and no more.

Both of these witnesses are discredited by the high character of Nora Burch.

There is much of pathetic force in the position which this
unfortunate woman, all unconscious of the condition, has
been forced to occupy in this trial. She is not here, and
cannot be here, to confront these witnesses, and stand up for
her virtue and her honor. Who will stand this day for the
virtue and the chastity of this poor unfortunate daughter of
the widow? I appeal to the manhood of this Board to
remember the testimony, the overwhelming testimony, as to
her character for purity and virtue, which has been given
on this trial by her neighbors at High Point, by the pure
and chaste maidens who have been her associate attendants
in this Institution, and to stand this day for the honor of
this widow's daughter.

What would be her suffering and her anguish, if she should
some day be restored to healthful mental condition, to learn
that during her days of darkness and utter helplessness, that
which was dearer to her than mental light or even life—
her character for purity and virtue—had been taken away
from her upon such evidence as you have heard in this speci-

fication. I know not how far Dr. Rogers may be guilty of the sins alleged against him ; but all good men will unite with me in saying that if, for the purpose of securing the downfall of a man whom he now hates, but who at one time was his best friend and his benefactor, he has been willing to involve the fair name of an unfortunate woman, and that the selection has been made for the reason that her affliction prevents her from coming here and speaking for her virtue and her honor, then he deserves the deepest condemnation.

Oh, how unfortunate is the position of this poor woman When Dr. Grissom, who is the only witness that can protect her against these vile charges, speaks for her honor, the counsel for the prosecution say that he is impeached on account of his great interest in the issue of this trial, and that you are not to believe him. The counsel for the prosecution who spoke yesterday said that the methods of mechanical restraint resorted to here were as cruel as the tortures of hell.; but if it be true that Nora Burch is a virtuous woman, then the conduct of this prosecution in relation to her is a thousand times more cruel than any act of restraint testified to by the most biased witness for the prosecution.

Why have they selected Nora Burch as the only one of the female attendants involved with Dr. Grissom in criminal intercourse? There have been a great many attendants in this Institution, and many handsome young women among them ; many of them, I take it, were equal in respect to physical charms to this widow's daughter, and yet against her, and her only, has this charge been made. Why was not this charge made before Nora Burch lost her reason? From the last of July, when, according to the witnesses, this act occurred, to the last of February, when she became insane, there was a period of seven months. I submit, that if the prosecution is the result of a conspiracy, if a shrewd leader would not conceive that it was safer, yea, necessary, to allege criminal intimacy with a woman who was dead or mentally incapable of testifying, and that, for the purpose of corroboration, by showing in evidence a general wicked and lecherous disposition on the part of the respondent, to procure females over whom he had acquired influence to testify to amorous advances and proposals for sinful connections by him, and their rejection by them, which would condemn him, and at the same time save their honor intact?

Then, next, gentlemen of the Board, we have the testimony of Dr. Grissom, which is an unequivocal denial of this criminal intercourse. Will you believe him? On the one hand, you have in his favor the high character that he has maintained among his fellow-men and the high position that he has held in the public confidence for nearly a quarter of a century. You have the testimony of Mrs. Lawrence and of Miss McKoy in his corroboration, and in impeachment of King and Jones. You have witnessed the bearing and demeanor of this old man on the witness stand, who in his life has now measured three score years of time. It was a trying ordeal to him; and yet his enemies cannot say, and the counsel for the prosecution did not say, bitter and denunciatory as he was of him, that he did not bear himself like a brave man, determined to tell the truth and nothing but the truth. He was not impeached by any cross-examination. The counsel for the prosecution, after he was turned over to them for examination, notwithstanding he had testified fully as to each and every charge and specification made against him, cross-examined him upon one point only, and that relating to another charge and specification and in no way relating to this charge or specification.

And on the other hand, Dr. Grissom is affected by his interest in the result of this trial, and it is for you, gentlemen, to say whether this is sufficient to outweigh the other considerations in his favor, and to lead your minds to the conclusion that he has sworn falsely.

You will pardon me for having taken up so much of your time in discussing this part of the case. My only excuse is,

2

that it is of so much consequence to him. It involves his future, not only of himself, but of those who are dearer to him than life. And, again, I assure you, that we are also striving for the vindication of the unfortunate widow's daughter. We appeal to your manhood to do her, as well as the respondent, justice. It is a rule of law, that you will not disregard, that a person charged before any court with any offence is supposed to be innocent until the contrary is proved.

Now, I submit to your judgment, with the responsibilities upon you, that you try this case according to the evidence: so help you, God. And let me implore you, that in considering the evidence, you will remember the silent witness now in the Morganton Asylum.

We come now to the second specification. It is that Dr. Grissom made amorous advances and lecherous proposals to Mrs. Perkinson. Mrs. Perkinson was never an attendant, nor in any way connected with the Institution as an employee, and therefore this specification had no proper place under this charge; but we realized that if that point had been made, it would have given to the uncharitable an occasion for saying that Dr. Grissom is seeking to avail himself of a mere technical defence, and to establish that if he has kept himself pure in relation to the female attendants of this Institution, he is not responsible to this Board for the morality of his conduct in relation to females outside of this Institution. So we meet this specification also, and deny it squarely.

It has been suggested that when Dr. Grissom admitted that, on one occasion, he was guilty of the impropriety of kissing Mrs. Perkinson under circumstances which appealed strongly to his sympathy, and so much so that Mrs. Perkinson herself admitted that she referred this act to an honorable motive, that he admitted the whole of this charge. Is it not true that a man cannot debauch every woman whom he may kiss?—nor does he expect to. I know that

there are numbers of men who take a different view; I am
glad that you do not belong to that class. I believe that,
among that class, any gallantry shown by a man to a woman,
however pure she may be, is referred to an unholy motive.
I am glad that I have a higher faith in the manhood and
womanhood of my people. It should be remembered to
Dr. Grissom's credit that, with the consciousness of how a
large number of people would view this act of indiscretion,
he admitted its truth. Why should he admit this and deny
the other acts which she testifies to, if they were all true?—for
this and all the rest were entirely dependent upon the uncorroborated testimony of Mrs. Perkinson. Dr. Grissom is a
man of experience, and he knew that when he testified to
that act of indiscretion how it might affect him—that even
those who would be charitable enough not to accept it as
proof of this charge, would allow it weight as affecting his
character for prudence. It was a terrible temptation upon him
to deny this act; many men who have occupied higher positions have fallen under the influence of a less temptation.
Who that is not in his position can appreciate this great
strain upon his moral nature? Persecuted by two of his
most important subordinates, upon charges which, if true,
would compass his utter ruin; one of these persecutors a
young man to whom he had stood almost as a father, fight-
ing him, according to his own admission, even to the death,
and the other, Mr. Thompson, the steward, a man of high
character, believing in his guilt, but, according to his testimony, not for anything he had seen that tended to prove
any immorality on his part, but actively and earnestly
engaged in the prosecution; and many of the other subordinates engaged in the combination for his overthrow—a colored servant who waited upon him made a prominent
witness against him. With all these things—and he fully
believed that a conspiracy had been formed for his overthrow—he saw that all of his conduct for the past few years
had been watched with suspicious eyes; that the friendship

of a long life had been attacked; that the whisper of slander had been busy with the name of a Christian woman, the widow of a dear friend—an old woman—and all because she had been faithful in her friendship, even to this end. He was standing in the face of this issue almost alone. Dr. Fuller, the first assistant physician, was too feeble in health to testify as to whether the matters alleged in these charges were true or not. It was a fearful crisis in his life, and that the old man stood there, burdened as he was, and spoke the truth and said, "I kissed Mrs. Perkinson," will be appreciated by brave men everywhere. You may convict him if you will, but he will carry with him to the grave the comforting reflection that in that hour God gave him strength to stand up for the truth. And yet there have been men so low, who were so thoroughly incapable of measuring any man by any higher standard than that they have prescribed for their own conduct, that they would say that if Dr. Grissom confessed to having kissed Mrs. Perkinson, he confessed to the whole. It is not in accordance with my taste or inclinations to attack a woman's reputation, and I shall make no attack upon Mrs. Perkinson. I will simply call your attention to the following facts: Mrs. Perkinson said she told her husband and her sister of the conduct of Dr. Grissom toward her; neither one of these came upon the stand to corroborate her. She continued to see Dr. Grissom after he had made the alleged improper advances to her, and her husband continued in the employment of Dr. Grissom without any protest or complaint to him of his conduct towards his wife. It may be argued that their necessitous condition compelled this conduct in order that her husband might have employment, but this does not explain why Mrs. Perkinson sent for Dr. Grissom to come to her house to see her sick child when she knew that she would be alone there except the child. Now, I do not mean to imply that Mrs. Perkinson had any improper motives, for I do not believe that she had, in sending for Dr. Grissom to come to see her child; but if Dr. Grissom had repeatedly made the attempts upon her virtue which she testified to, it is hardly consistent with the high character which has been given her by witnesses on this stand that she should have asked Dr. Grissom to visit her sick child, when there were so many other physicians living close by, and Dr. Fuller and Dr. Rogers were equally as near as Dr. Grissom.

I proceed now to the specification which alleges improper advances and proposals by the respondent to Miss Edwards. In view of the very exhaustive argument made by Col. Fuller in considering this part of the case, and in discussing what weight should be given to the testimony of Miss Edwards, I shall not discuss at length the evidence that was offered upon this specification. The only evidence which the prosecution offered was the testimony of Miss Edwards herself. She testified that Dr. Grissom, on more than one occasion, attempted to kiss her and to induce her to sit in his lap, and that on one occasion he attempted to take liberties with her person while she was lying sick in bed. That he proposed, first, if she would yield to his wishes, that he would abandon his wife, whom, she declared, he said he had not loved for many years, and flee with her. She said that she rejected this proposition ; and then she testified that he offered, if she would yield to his solicitations, to make her the matron of the Institution ; and she said the last time he offered these indignities to her was when she went into his office the last day she was at the Institution, in March, 1888, and that she then informed him that she had received a telegram calling her home on account of the extreme illness of her mother, and that on account of his conduct to her she would never return to the Institution. She admitted that she had been in correspondence with Dr. Rogers, and had met him once in Greensboro since she left here.

Dr. Grissom testified that he had never made any improper advances to her either by word or conduct, and he denied specifically every one of the allegations which she made against him. The Rev. Mr. Whitaker testified that, on the day on which she left this Institution, he traveled with her on the cars as far as Merry Oaks, in Chatham County, and during that time he engaged her in conversation, and she spoke in the very highest terms of Dr. Grissom, and said that it was her purpose, whether her mother lived or died, to return to the Institution. Mr. Whitaker further testified, that she spoke in very high terms of Dr. Rogers, and that he told her that he expected that she and Dr. Rogers were sweethearts, and to this remark she simply smiled.

You will remember, gentlemen, the testimony of Mrs. Williams. She said that Miss Edwards visited her in her home in the city of Raleigh; that Dr. Rogers called to see her there, and that Miss Edwards introduced Dr. Rogers to the witness as Mr. Edwards, a relative of hers. She further testified that, on one occasion, at night, when Dr. Rogers called to see Miss Edwards, they were standing out in the porch, that she opened the door to invite them into the house, and she discovered that Dr. Rogers had his arm around Miss Edwards' waist. I call your attention to the coincidence that the evidence of Miss Edwards was like in kind, and almost in expression, to the directions given by Dr. Rogers in his letter, which has been offered in evidence, written to another female friend as to the facts she should testify to concerning Dr. Grissom's conduct towards her.

It is not my purpose to speak harshly of Miss Edwards. Witnesses from her own home have testified to her good character. I shall not seek to impeach her character for chastity or virtue, but I think it is fairly deducible, from the evidence, that she was decidedly under the influence of Dr. Rogers, and has shared in his bitter feeling toward Dr. Grissom. I think her conduct calls for the exercise of pity rather than severe criticism, for she was under the influence of a young man to whom she was attached, and in whom she greatly trusted; and I think I am warranted, from the evidence, in stating that she has testified in accordance with his wishes, if not his directions. The counsel for the prosecution present her as an unsophisticated young woman from the country, without experience, and without guile. As affecting the value of her testimony, I refer you to her conduct and bearing as a witness. When this artless young girl came into this room, and was going to place her hand upon the Bible to be sworn as a witness, she clenched her fan in her right hand and defiantly shook it at the respondent. Was this evidence of very great modesty? Would not the typical maiden of our Southland, if she were called upon to testify before a court of gentlemen concerning such charges as are the issues in this trial, and to such facts as Miss Edwards had come to testify to, be so affected by a feeling of shame and personal mortification that she would have approached the witness-stand with faltering steps and downcast eyes? During the progress of her examination as a witness, Dr. Grissom whispered something to his own counsel, when she spoke out with considerable show of feeling, and said, " Oh, he will tell a lie in a minute;" and again during her examination, and speaking to the counsel of Dr. Grissom, and not in response to any question by them, she said : " Dr. Grissom is mean enough to do anything." Was that deportment consistent with modesty? Certainly, if an artist had been seeking for a model for a statue to represent modesty, he would have passed that young woman by on that occasion.

Is it not strange, gentlemen, that this young, modest woman should have experienced these wicked wrongs from Dr. Grissom, and failed to have communicated with some lady friend in relation thereto? She says she did not tell her father, because she did not want him to take Dr. Grissom's life. She was neither too modest, nor so much concerned for the safety of Dr. Grissom, that she did not communicate them to Dr. Rogers and to the counsel for the prosecution, even when she knew the purpose for which they were to be used. It seems to me, that a modest maiden, if she had kept this secret for twelve months, would never have given it away with a knowledge that the result would be its publication in a trial. But I will say no more of this young woman, for it is clear that she was dominated in respect to her conduct in this trial by the will of Dr. Rogers.

What shall I say of Dr. Rogers? I will not indulge in any very severe denunciation of him. I am full of regret at his conduct. Oh, if he had only submitted himself to the dictates of prudence and discretion and a virtuous ambition—if he could have discarded whatever was sensual, low and unworthy, and striven for that which was grand, noble and enduring, he would have had not only the respect of his contemporaries, but he might have written his name so high that all men might have read it. A few years ago his life was full of promise. He bears an honored name—it is the name of his father, who was much respected and honored in North Carolina. He had no need to be ashamed of that name, that he should visit one of the female attendants of this Institution under an assumed name; but he may well be ashamed of the man who bears that name. The people of North Carolina are not ashamed of that name, but they are full of shame and mortification on account of the man who now bears it, for whose honor they had vouched by giving him so responsible a position. Why, if Dr. Rogers' intentions were honorable, did he not call on this woman openly, and send up his card with his own name on it? The truth is, that Dr. Rogers is an intriguer; he bobs up frequently during the history developed by this trial, and wherever you see him he is intriguing; wherever you strike his foot-prints, they are on a scheming errand, whether it be in the house of Mrs. Perkinson, when he talks with her about Dr. Grissom's conduct towards her, and tells her that he has treated others in the same way, and that she must go to Raleigh that night and tell it to his lawyers; whether it be when he is writing the long letter to his female friend, the first four pages of which are full of passionate expressions, that she might be moved thereby to comply with his request, contained in the last pages of the letter, to furnish such evidence as he suggested would be helpful to enable him to "down the old scoundrel," with whom he was about to engage in a fight to the very death; or whether it be in calling on Miss Edwards at the residence of Miss Williams, under an assumed name; or whether it be in procuring the attendance of the employees of this Institution, before this prosecution was commenced, at the office of an attorney in the city of Raleigh;—wherever he is, at all times and in all places, he is scheming and intriguing. If Dr. Rogers had not allowed his feelings, and his desire to "down the old scoundrel," to override his judgment, it would not have escaped him that the history of this world has taught that, scheme as you will and intrigue as you may, manufactured testimony has rarely succeeded in accomplishing its purpose. It almost always happens that the greatest caution and forethought has been unequal to the task of completing the entire wall and guarding every point. It has always been so—it will always be so. It will so turn out that some fact will be clearly established that will be inconsistent with the alleged material facts and the theory of the conspiracy, and when this is so, the whole must fall to the ground. For it is true that every fact in this universe must be in harmony with every other fact, and the attempt to establish as a fact, that which is not a fact, is, as it were, an effort to disharmonize the universe.

The fact that the Rev. Mr. Whitaker rode on the train with Miss Edwards in March, 1888, and had a conversation with her, and the nature of the conversation seemed unimportant at the time, but what Miss Edwards said in that conversation, which, doubtless, she never expected to hear of again, and which Dr. Rogers never knew of, has been very important in this case.

There are two other specifications under this charge of immorality—the one alleging amorous advances by the respondent towards Miss Morris, the other alleging the same conduct on his part towards Miss Rosa Bryant—but the prosecution did not introduce any evidence in support of either one of these charges. It is to be deprecated that the names of these ladies should have been made to figure in these charges, thus, in some measure, reflecting upon their honor without a particle of evidence to justify it.

I shall now proceed to the second charge: That Dr. Grissom, Superintendent of this Institution, has been guilty of mismanagement and cruel treatment of the patients under his charge. It was upon this charge that the counsel for the prosecution made his speech on yesterday. In the course of his remarks, he said that exalted position would not protect a man from the consequences of his evil-doing. That is true; and it is equally true that virtue forms no shield to ward off the arrows of calumny, and that exalted position, however worthily filled, does not prevent the attacks of jealousy, but rather induces them. The counsel was rather facetious in his references to the observations which Col. Fuller made upon the high character of Dr. Grissom; but is it not true that Dr. Grissom has proven himself to be a man of high character? Has he not held for twenty-one years the high position which he now fills? And may you not take notice of these things in determining the value of this testimony, if for no other purpose? It is not claimed that he is the greatest representative of his profession in North Carolina, nor that he is the only man capable of filling the office he holds, for there are, I am glad to say, many members of his profession in this State who would fill well this high place. We have not claimed that he is exempt from the weaknesses of human nature which belong to all of us, nor that he is above sinning. It has not been intimated by us that he should not be tried by the same rules that would obtain in the trial of the humblest citizen of the land. It has seemed to us right, and we have said so, that he should have a fair trial upon the evidence, and that whatever of character he or his witnesses have, ought to be considered in estimating the weight and value of the testimony of the defence. It is to be regretted that, on this trial, the purpose of which is to depose from his high position a person who has hitherto been held in high esteem by the public, and who is impeached only by the charges and the evidence in this trial, all of which is controverted, the counsel for the prosecution, in respect to his sense of duty to his cause, has felt called upon to indulge in such bitter denunciation of the unfortunate respondent. With great respect, and disclaiming any intention of assuming a right to criticise the conduct of their prosecution, I declare to you that I do not think the expressions of denunciation and of abuse which fell from the counsel's lips were justified by the aspect of this case. It cannot be insisted, for justification of his course, that we have not been careful of our utterances in relation to Dr. Rogers' conduct. Their cases are different. Dr. Rogers, according to his own written declaration, has been guilty of conduct deserving of the severest condemnation. He is a volunteer prosecutor in this action, and has been actively engaged therein, and yet he has refused to go upon the stand and testify as a witness, so that we might have the opportunity of cross-examining him. On the other hand, Dr. Grissom has, in obedience to a legal requirement arising upon the preferring of these charges, appeared for the purpose of answering and defending himself against them. There has been no proof of any written or unwritten declaration on his part of any fact tending to prove him guilty of any one of the charges. There has been evidence tending to prove him guilty of each one of the charges, and there has been evidence in rebuttal for his defence as to every one of them.

If it is a fact that the question of his guilt as to every one of the charges is still open, is he to be denounced as a criminal? Is there nothing in his past; is there nothing in his conduct and bearing on the stand as a witness; is there nothing in the gray hairs of an old age that has hitherto been honorable; and could not all of these avail to shield him against the expressions of contempt and denunciation?

The counsel, among other things, said : "Allow Dr. Grissom to remain here, and he will soon tie up a man by the thumbs if he does not act in accordance with his wishes." Upon what authority does he say this? There is no evidence to warrant any such conclusion. He invoked God, then he attempted to call up the ghosts and to call down the spirits, and then he prayed a prayer. It was the Lord's prayer. Yes, standing there, and after indulging in the most fearful denunciations of the respondent, he raised his hands on high, and uttered the sublime language contained in the beautiful prayer : "Forgive us our trespasses, as we forgive those who trespass against us." Did it never occur to him that the conception of the divine mind was that this prayer should have, not only expression, but a spirit also? Does he not remember that it is said of the circumstances under which this prayer is to be uttered, that "thou shalt not be as the hypocrites; for they love to pray standing in the synagogues and in the corners of the streets, that they may be seen of men. Verily, I say unto you, they have their reward. But when thou prayest, enter into thy closet, and when thou hast shut thy door, pray to thy Father which is in secret, and thy Father which seeth in secret shall reward thee openly."

But there was a prayer which he might have uttered, and which, if he will pardon me for saying so, would have been more in accord with the spirit of this prosecution; and it is this: "Oh! Lord, I thank Thee that I am not as other men, especially this poor old gray-haired Superintendent of the North Carolina Insane Asylum."

This part of his speech calls to my mind an incident which occurred in the western part of the State. There was a pious old woman who belonged to a church with a small membership, in a remote section, and she did not often have an opportunity of hearing preaching; but on one occasion it was appointed that a preacher of considerable reputation would fill the pulpit of her little church. She invited some of her friends to come and hear the preacher, and coupled it with invitations to dine with her after the service was over. Her friends came, and the preacher came, but he failed to come up to expectations in his sermon. When the friends of the old woman were gathered with her around the dinner-table, they engaged in pretty sharp criticisms upon the sermon. The old woman listened in silence for a while, and then, turning to them with an appealing look, she said: " Well, brethren, I will admit that he didn't preach much of a sermon, but you are bound to allow that he was monstrous shifty in pray'r."

Much of the evidence upon this second charge, and the specifications thereunder, was upon the propriety of mechanical restraint as a method of treatment for certain classes of insane, and much of the argument of counsel was directed to the same matter. It seems to us that the fact that the Board of Directors have recognized this method of treatment in the By-Laws of the Institution would be sufficient justification for its use by the Superintendent of the Institution. But suppose that this were not so, the question of mechanical restraint or non-restraint, according to the evidence, is still within the field of controversy. The English rule is against mechanical restraint; the American rule is in favor of it; and to each of these rules you will find exceptions in each of the countries.

But the question is dependent for a settlement in this Institution upon a law that neither you nor I have the power to contravene. It is the law of necessity. The annual appropriation to this Institution is $55,000, which would be totally inadequate to support this Institution, with the number of patients here, if mechanical restraint were abolished. The violent insane must, at times, be restrained by some power to prevent them from doing injury to themselves or to others. If mechanical restraint is to be abolished, then you must increase the number of attendants here by so many as would afford a sufficient number of attendants to follow after and continually watch each of the violent insane. This would require a larger appropriation than the State of North Carolina has made to this Institution, or is able to make, or else the reducing of the number of the inmates of this Asylum to about one-third of its present number. The General Assembly of the State has settled this question by the amount of its appropriation. The Board of Directors of this Asylum has settled this question by allowing so many inmates in this Institution that, within the appropriation, the Superintendent of the Institution would not be free to elect as between the system of restraint and non-restraint.

The counsel for the prosecution referred you to the Indiana Insane Asylum, in which mechanical restraint has been abolished, and he discussed the report of the superintendent of that institution as illustrating the beneficial effects of the change; but he did not tell you that the annual appropriation to that institution, as stated in the very book that contains that report, is $260,000.

It often happens that there are inmates of this Institution who belong to the class known as the criminally insane. They are those who have been indicted by a grand jury, and on their arraignment for trial before a petit jury have pleaded "insanity," and the jury has found that they were insane, and they have been, by order of the court, transferred to this Asylum. According to the evidence, of those to whom it is alleged that Dr. Grissom has been cruel in his treatment, one was indicted for rape, one for arson, and one for an assault with a deadly weapon.

Insanity is not a loss of the mind, but it is a disease of the mind, and many of the patients here have homicidal tendencies, and some have suicidal tendencies. Because the appropriation made to this Institution will not allow the employment of sufficient attendants to watch over and restrain these men in their violent paroxysms, are the poor,

weak, helpless and innocent insane here to be in peril of
their lives or bodily harm, or are these violent insane to be
mechanically restrained? That is the question. It is not
difficult to criticise the methods of an institution, but it is
quite another thing to adopt others that are better, and that
are possible and consistent with already fixed, stated conditions. Would it be wise policy to abolish mechanical restraint
in this Institution at the cost of sending two-thirds of the
inmates back to the places from whence they came—some
of them to the common jails of their counties, and some of
them to homes in which there is a struggle, even now, without the additional burden they would bring, to keep want
and suffering for bread outside the threshold? And remember that if this were done, of those who remained here would
be the criminally insane. That is fixed by the orders of the
courts.

Dr. Grissom testified that the application of mechanical
restraint is, in some cases, proper and necessary treatment,
and that in the cases where he resorted to it, it was, according to his best judgment, proper treatment for the patient.
The counsel for the prosecution insists that this cannot be
so, for that, according to the testimony of witnesses, several
of the patients were restrained because of acts of violence
towards the Superintendent or others of the Institution.

It may be that the witnesses and the counsel have fallen
into the error of referring the mechanical restraints to facts
as causes, instead of evidences or symptoms of the nervous
and mental conditions of the patient which, to an alienist
like Dr. Grissom, made such treatment proper.

Now, it was testified by one of the witnesses that one of
the patients, named in one of the specifications, and a man
of violent disposition and homicidal mania, on one occasion
when Dr. Grissom passed through the ward, followed him,
abusing him and attempting acts of violence upon him, and
for this he said Dr. Grissom ordered him to be restrained.
The truth is, that the conduct of the patient discovered a

mental condition requiring restraint, both in respect to his own safety and the safety of other patients in the ward. Dr. Grissom must not be held responsible for the fact that an attendant has not the learning to appreciate a scientific deduction from given facts.

If we were as ignorant of the treatment of physical diseases as we are of mental diseases, doubtless many times we would think that our family physician was cruel in the use of remedial agents. A physician is called to see a patient who is suffering from the effects of a determination of the blood to the brain. He attempts to feel the pulse of the patient, the patient strikes at him, and, in his delirium, calls him bad names; the physician directly thereafter, with his lancet, cuts into the arm of the patient and lets out a quantity of blood. An ignorant servant concludes that the doctor cut the patient as a punishment for striking at him and using bad language; but that does not make it so.

In the case referred to above, and alleged against Dr. Grissom for cruelty, was it better that Dr. Grissom should go out of the ward after he had completed his visit, and leave that patient in a violent temper, which would most probably have found vent in a forcible attack upon some of the other patients, or was it better to have him restrained? The one course was consistent with his own safety and convenience; the other was consistent with duty and the safety of the other patients.

The cases of alleged cruelty to the female patients, excepting the case of Mrs. Lowter, depend entirely upon the evidence of Miss Edwards; and in view of the fact that she is uncorroborated, and that Dr. Grissom, who testifies that he was not guilty of the acts alleged, is corroborated in important particulars, I shall not discuss at any length those specifications. The testimony of Miss Edwards, that the Superintendent, on one occasion, as a punishment to two of the female patients who had been engaged in a fight, locked them together in a room and left them to fight it out, and

33

that they did fight for a long while, and to the extent of four fully bruising each other, and that Dr. Grissom watched them for a while through the trap-door and seemed to enjoy the conflict, needs corroboration. It cannot be that this unusual incident could have occurred in any ward of this Institution without attracting the attention of some of the others, and, being the subject of remark among all, of the attendants of this Institution. It is presuming too much against the intelligent judgment of these triers to ask that they should believe that a conflict should have been waged between two infuriated insane women, with the approval of the Superintendent, without attracting the attention of any other attendant or servant of this Institution besides Miss Edwards; and yet not one other testifies to any knowledge or information of that fact. And of the witnesses examined, touching Dr. Grissom's treatment of those patients, all denied any information or knowledge thereof.

The act of cruelty alleged to have been committed against Miss Foy was the dashing of cold water in her face. Dr. Grissom admitted that he did this, but that he did it as a method of treatment. He says that Miss Foy was a very excitable patient, and that he had discovered that, in her case, and with some other patients who were suffering with paroxysms of excitement and a disposition to violence, by dashing, suddenly, cold water into the face it would produce a mental impression that would be beneficial in reducing the excitement of the patient. He says one peculiarity of this patient was that she imagined herself the wife of Dr. Rogers, and that she would sometimes seize hold of Dr. Rogers as he went through her ward.

The counsel for the prosecution was pleased, in his argument, to refer to the treatment of Miss Foy as a desire on the part of Dr. Grissom to punish her on account of her expressions of attachment and affection for Dr. Rogers, whom he so much hated. Can it be that the counsel believes this? Is there any evidence to warrant any such statement? Dr.

3

Grissom can't be so vile as that, for a man vile and wicked enough to do that thing could not for these past years so have veiled his real character from the world. I sincerely trust that there is not a member of this Board, whatever may be his conclusion upon the issues of this trial, who will do Dr. Grissom the injustice—the gross injustice—to believe that he was inspired by so low and vile a motive.

In relation to the charge of choking the patient Henry Cone, Dr. Grissom says that he was, at times, a very excitable, a very violent and a very dangerous patient; that he had a habit of springing suddenly on one; that when he was in one of these paroxysms, there would be a great rush of blood to his face and head; that his eyes would become bloodshot; that on the occasion referred to in the specification he was in a condition of great excitement, and that he sprang upon him suddenly and with great violence; that he threw him off, and that, after that, he put one hand on either side of his neck and pressed on the carotid arteries, and this was to prevent the great rush of blood to the brain; that he did not choke him. There is a carotid artery on either side of the neck, which takes the blood to the brain, and, sometimes, by the application of pressure on these arteries, the flow of blood to the brain may be lessened, and beneficial effects follow. And this was true in Henry Cone's case. Dr. Grissom did not explain to the attendant why he was pressing on the patient's neck; he was not called upon to do that, and the attendant thought, from the position of his hands, that he was choking the patient. But if his explanation to this Board is satisfactory, he is therewith content. I have no doubt but that his explanation is satisfactory, and his conduct in this respect justified by the gentlemen of the medical profession on this Board.

In the case of Mrs. Lowter, the counsel insists that her death was in consequence of the restraint imposed upon her by order of the Superintendent. Not one witness who testified for the prosecution, or for the defence, according to my recollection, agreed with the counsel Those who testified as to this specification, agreed that Mrs. Lowter appeared as well after she had been freed from restraint as she ever had been. Mrs. V. C. Jones, who was for eighteen years an attendant in this Institution, and was a long while the chief attendant, and a woman of high character, testified to this fact.

The counsel was surely mistaken in stating that Mrs. Lowter was restrained because she would not take her bath. In describing the character or form of her insanity and its manifestations, one of the witnesses said that Mrs. Lowter was a very peculiar and contrary patient; that she would not submit to directions in any particular; that she would not yield to solicitations or requests; and, among other things, the witness said that she would not take a bath or go to her meals, unless she was compelled thereto by force. Dr. Grissom testified that Mrs. Lowter was in such a condition of excitement that he ordered her restrained, thinking it best and necessary for the purpose of composing her.

In relation to the specification of cruelty to Upchurch, it appears, from the evidence, that he was one of the criminally insane. Before he was sent here, he had shot his brother, and had made an attempt against the life of another man. He was a very violent and very dangerous patient. He had torn a piece of iron from the window and was threatening violence and defying the attendants. Dr. Grissom was sent for, and when he came, he found the patient in a great rage, and brandishing the iron bar. He directed that he should be disarmed and restrained. One of the attendants proposed to go in the room with a stick and disarm him; this, Dr. Grissom forbade, but, under his direction, the attendants took a mattress and, holding it before them, rushed upon him, pressed him against the wall and threw him upon the floor and disarmed him. There was a great struggle, and Dr. Grissom testifies that he, the attendants, and Mr. Thompson, were very much excited. Mr. Thompson stood in the

door, but did not aid in disarming or controlling the patient.
Dr. Grissom, according to his testimony, while Upchurch
was on the floor and struggling with the attendants, went up
and put his foot on the upper part of Upchurch's body,
about the shoulder or neck. One of the other witnesses,
Harris, I think, says he put his foot in his face. Mr. Thompson, and at least one other witness, and probably two, say
that he stamped him in the face, and that afterwards there
was blood on the corner of his mouth; and several of the
witnesses say that Dr. Grissom, at that time, cursed Upchurch;
but all agree that no serious injury was done to Upchurch.

It is admitted that the force used in this case was not limited by its necessity, but we insist that it was not done with
any cruel purpose, but was the result of impulse upon excitement. If you shall have at the head of this Institution a
man who is qualified for the place, he will sometimes do
wrong. It is the strong man who occasionally commits
wrong; it is only the weak "goody-goody" sort who are
safe against this danger—but their daily life and conduct
are made up of the sins of omission. It would not be consistent with the necessity that is upon us all to ask for a
charitable construction upon our past conduct to hold that
for this one act of wrong this respondent, as Superintendent
of this Institution, is guilty of cruel treatment to the patients
of this Institution.

The discussion of the other specifications under this
charge, and of the third charge, and the specifications thereunder, will be left to my associates who follow me.

And now, gentlemen of the Board, I trust that I may
again, without offence to you, urge upon you that this case
is to be tried according to the evidence. One of the counsel
for the prosecution during the conduct of this trial has stated
that this respondent is on trial before two tribunals—the one
is this Board, and the other the million and a half people of
North Carolina. That may be so; it certainly is true that
the people of North Carolina feel great interest in this trial.

I know not what may be their verdict upon the issues, but I do say this, that your opinion of what may be the popular judgment upon these charges must not affect your judgment upon the evidence. And the intelligent people of North Carolina who love justice and fair play, and who have delegated to you the power for this trial, would not ask that you should be guided and directed by anything else but your own intelligent apprehension of, and conscientious regard for, the evidence, and the whole evidence.

I have tried to discuss the evidence fairly, and to state it in substance correctly. If, in my zeal for my client, I have failed in this, your own judgment and recollection will not be at fault. We have striven in this trial, not only for an acquittal of the respondent, but for his vindication, certainly in respect to the charge upon morality. We have confidence that, upon the evidence upon this charge of immorality, each and every member of this Board will vote for his acquittal, for anything less than that would not entirely free him from the stain.

For your patient hearing of me, I thank you.

www.ingramcontent.com/pod-product-compliance
Lightning Source LLC
Chambersburg PA
CBHW021451090426
42739CB00009B/1711